Debating To Win Arguments

The Elements of Debating, and How to Counter Arguments With Ease Using Logic

R. L. Greene

The information in the following pages is broadly considered to be a truthful and accurate account of facts, and as such any inattention, use or misuse of the information in question by the reader will render any resulting actions solely under their purview. There are no scenarios in which the publisher or the original author of this work can be in any fashion deemed liable for any hardship or damages that may befall them after undertaking information described herein.

Additionally, the information found on the following pages is intended for informational purposes only and should thus be considered, universal. As befitting its nature, the information presented is without assurance regarding its continued validity or interim quality. Trademarks that mentioned are done without written consent and can in no way be considered an endorsement from the trademark holder.

ISBN: 978-0-9987936-5-8

TABLE OF CONTENTS

INTRODUCTION 6

WHAT IS YOUR MOOT 8

ELEMENTS OF DEBATE.. 14

WHAT IS FALSE EQUIVALENCY.................................... 19

THE DIFFERENCE BETWEEN FACT & OPINION 23

THE DIFFERENCE BETWEEN SUBJECTIVE & OBJECTIVE....27

HOW TO DISSECT OPPOSING VIEW.............................33

STATISTIC & HOW THEY CAN BE MANIPULATED................. 50

HOW TO USE OPPOSING ARGUMENT LOGIC AGAINST THEM 65

CONCLUSION 69

INTRODUCTION

Debating, we do it every day. Some of us are better at it than others. I hope you want to be one of those better ones. That is why you read this book, to gain an edge on improving the articulation of your opinions. Think back to a time when you had an opposing view of someone, and you knew you were right, but just couldn't say the right words to prove your point. Or when you went for a job interview. You had to convince your employer you are the best candidate for the job. Guess what, you were debating in an informal way for both of those scenarios.

Communication on varying views, which is frequently accomplished in a formal manner, is known as debate. When debating, you share facts, and or opinion to convince your audience or even the opposition that your arguments are more substantial.

Debating is a craft that is learnable. We all already have most prerequisites to succeed in the art of debating. It might be the case that some of your skills might require development to better prepare yourself to refute an argument. That is why Debating To Win Arguments is written; to assist ordinary folks, in achieving the extraordinary; when they enter into the magnificent craft of debating. Before we begin, I will give a disclaimer. This book may delve deep in the science of debating, but this is a necessary to hone this skill, as it will show to be beneficial throughout life.

CHAPTER 1

WHAT IS YOUR MOOT

M oot is sometimes used to state the topic open for discussion or debate. Either you agree on the moot, or you disagree with the moot. If you are opposing the moot then, you must provide your rebuttal of the moot.

Good right, you see learning about the craft of debating is not as hard as you had initially thought.

Oh, one quick fact though before we continue; never confuse *mute* with *moot*. Once it has anything to do with a discussion or a debate *moot* is the word used. Even if your ears transmit *mute* to your brain, tell your brain that your ears heard the wrong word. *Mute* deals with the silencing of something. For example, you put your television on *mute,* or you *mute* the stereo in your car, or you mute your cellular phone. So, *moot* we discuss, and *mute* "Shhhh!" it is quiet time, for you stopped the sound by muting the device or your statement have muted someone.

Debate, like other artistries, has jargons. Jargons are particular words used by certain groups, and if someone is not a part of that group, they might not understand the words used by the group members. To explain jargons in a different way, they are the secret codes a group uses that others might not understand, unless, a member of the group teaches them the meaning of the words. Or like in your case, you can purchase a book to learn about the group's jargon.

Therefore, the first step in the improvement of your prerequisites for debating is learning the jargon used by debaters.

Okay, it is time to learn how to talk the talk, and later you will learn how to walk the walk. I will share with some words or jargon you must know; because they are frequently used in debates.

I told you about moot earlier, but you will also hear some debaters use the word *motion* to refer to the statement or the topic of debate. Moot meaning has changed over the years, and in American English, it means "Pointless." However, in British English, it still carries the meaning "To debate." Always consider your audience before using *moot*. To be on the safer side you can opt to use the word *motion. Resolution* is another word some debaters will use to refer to the statement of value or policy being argued. Throughout this book the word *motion* will refer to the debate's topic.

To conduct a debate, you must have more than one individuals involved. Two people can debate a motion, or you might have two teams debating a motion. One individual or one team agrees on the motion and is the *affirmative* or the *proposition* side. The side in disagreement is called the *negative* or the *opposition*.

The a*rgument*, the evidence presented in speeches, acting as proof of their support, will refute the opposition's statements with the affirmative or proposition side. With the negative or opposition, the *argument* is the evidence presented to disprove, and whatever evidence the affirmative presented.

Definition, this is stating the central word(s) or individual(s) in the motion. *Interpretation* explains the importance of the motion. Both the *definition* and the *interpretation* are usually outlined by the first speaker of both the affirmative and negative side.

The *presentation* is how the speakers demonstrate or display their arguments. Speakers, presentation are mainly through speech with gesticulations, tone, volume, pitch, and rhythm. *Modulation* can describe the tone, volume, pitch and rhythm of their voice.

Structure refers to the format of each speaker's speech and how well each speaker's argument correlates to his/her team members.

Protected time is the first sixty seconds and the last sixty seconds of a debate that the speaker must speak without interruption from the opposing speakers.

Points of information or PoI this is during the speech of a speaker, a speaker from the opposing side interjects to offer a brief, quick rebuttal to the point(s) made by the speaker who is presenting.

Barrack is to offer a succession of quick points of information, which are usually disruptive when done in that manner.

Rebuttal is the statements or explanation that dispute the arguments of the other team.

A *strike* is when a judge is prohibited from adjudicating a team due to the potential bias by that person.

Taking brief notes of critical points raised in arguments in a debate, by both the judges, and each team involved in the debate is *flowing*.

An *open round* is when the adjudication results are announced to teams after the debate.

However, in a *closed round,* this is when the adjudication results are kept a secret from the teams.

The *opening opposition* is the first speaker on the side of the opposition with the responsibility to presenting arguments against the motion and the rebuttal of the opening proposition.

The *room* is the physical location where the debated is conducted.

The allocation of points of the individual speakers during a debate, which is generally awarded based on their speech is *speaker points* or *speaks.* The maximum point awarded to individual speakers is one hundred.

Team points are the points allocated to teams for their performance during the debate. These points will determine which team wins the debate.

Squirrel is the attempt by the opening proposition to illicitly and irrationally restrict the motion.

The *summation* is the closing speech from both the proposition and the opposition, which summarizes the debate.

The person responsible for creating and sustaining the *tab,* and the draw throughout, and after the debating competition is called a *tabmaster.*

The *tab* is the overall ranking of judges and speakers in a debating competition.

Hey! Give yourself a tap on the shoulder. I am very proud of you for reading this far. Now, buckle up because you are about to take another step on the ladder *"Debating To Win Arguments"* in your quest to become a better debater. See you on the next page.

CHAPTER 2

ELEMENTS OF DEBATE

Relax; you have made it to chapter two. We will discuss the elements of debate in this chapter. I want you to perceive debate like a game, a game you will enjoy playing. In this game, your aim is to win like all other games. So, you must study your opponent, and anticipate what that competitor next move will be. Wellwith debate, it is the opposition arguments. You must learn the roles of the players in the game and what you must do to win.

Every game has rules, and each player has a value too. In the game of debate, players are the elements that make a debate possible. Each element has a significant role, and I will discuss their individual roles below:

One main rule in the game of debate is that you must adhere to the boundary of the game. Let us think of debate like basketball. Players may not step on or pass the sideline when dribbling the ball. If a player breaches the rule of the sideline while dribbling, the opponent gets the ball. The sideline in each game of debate is set by the motion. The team that does not breach the motion, and present the most substantial arguments based on their claim of the motion; stands a greater chance of being declared the winner.

Stick to the motion. Let it come alive in your arguments. Even if you must debate something that personally, you do not agree with, in the game of debate, you make the judge(s) or the audience believes that the motion is one of your solemn beliefs. So, you must try to define the motion, state why you believe it is important, and look for ways to refute whatever negatives your opponent will argue about the motion. Or, if you are in the opposition, you must find negatives to refute whatever positive the proposition will claim. Whatever side of the coin you fall on, when you are on a debate team, just remember to research points that will solidify your claims to the motion.

Here is a very tricky and special key element to the game of debate, one which some debaters forget. Keep your eyes on the judge. Okay, this is no joke. You literally must keep your eyes on the judge. If you were one of the individuals that think that in a debate, the individuals do not face each other; because it will help them not be nervous when presenting their speeches; you were very wrong for thinking that way.

You are there to convince the judge of your claims about the motion and not the opponent. If it is possible to know who will be the judging the debate before the appointed time for the debate can be an asset for you. You could research about the adjudication style of the judge. By researching the judging format of the judge, you could structure your arguments in the preferred format of the presiding judge.

It is time to pick a side. Now, I think I can convince you; that I was not joking, when I said that debate is like a game. Every game has sides, right. Yes, the next element in the game of debating is the sides. Whether you are a part of a team, or you are debating against another individual, you must select a side. You are either on the affirmative or on the negative side.

Tick-tock, tick-tock, you better keep watch on the hands of the clock, for the next element in the game of debating is the speeches. Each speaker must present their argument in timed rounds, with very distinctive rules. For example, one rule is the protected time when the speaker must present with no interruption from the opponent. Then, there is the point of information when the opponent might ask permission of the speaker presenting to give a brief rebuttal. The speaker presenting has the option to refuse the request from the opponent.

A point of order is raised when an opponent thinks that the speaker breached one rule of the debate. A point of order is only permitted under these two situations: the first situation is if a speaker presenting has exceeded his or her allotted time, and the second is the introduction of a new argument during the either of the two rebuttal speeches. For an opponent to raise a point of order, he or she must get up from his or her seat and say; "Point of order."

The speaker presenting will stop his or her speech. Then, the individual that raised the point of order will state which rule(s) is violated. He or she will say; "The speaker is over time" or "The speaker just made a new argument (state what is the new argument that the speaker made) in the rebuttal."

The speaker given the task of judging the debate will say; "Point well taken" if he or she agrees with the point of order. This means that if the speaker presenting had exceeded his or her time that speaker must conclude his or her speech. And, if it was a new argument introduced, that new argument will not be considered. However, if he or she does not agree with the point of order the response given is; "Not well taken." If the point of order is not well taken the debater may continue presenting and for a new argument it will be considered.

You must practice the time for presenting your speech before the day of the competition; this will assist in building your confidence, and ensure you can adhere to your allotted time. Speeches will be timed and you must stop when your assigned time is finished.

A moment for drum roll please, for it is decision time, the next element in the game of debate. The debate is over and teams or individuals anxiously await the results. During the decision, the debaters will know if their arguments hit the goal net in the minds of the judge(s) or audience. One team will be declared the winner and one the loser. Individual speakers will know what their speaker points are and teams will be told their team points.

Awesome, you are doing great; because you have just learned the five elements to make a debate possible. Yes, I said five elements. That is pretty remarkable for a game in which you will unearth a wealth of knowledge, wisdom, and experience while you learn how to communicate more effectively.

Reader, I support the claim that you will continue reading *Debating To Win Arguments* which can help you become a better debater.

CHAPTER 3

WHAT IS FALSE EQUIVALENCY

False equivalency is like the story regarding the numeral six and the numeral nine. If you are looking at the nine when turn up-side down it looks like a six, and if you turn the numeral six the wrong way it looks like a nine.

So, take for instance a large numeral nine was placed between two persons, who are standing and facing each other. To one of individuals the nine will look like a six, and to the other individual it is a nine. Both individuals will provide logic arguments they are correct. However, only one is really correct.

False equivalency is just that logic with fallacy between two opposing arguments. The logical equivalency is usually validated based on the quality or quantity of the evidence being presented.

Take for example people who hold the belief that killing is wrong. They will say whoever kills, has committed murder, and must pay the penalty of imprisonment. Say a suicide bomber had gotten the chance to place a bomb in an airport, set off the bomb, and then manage to escape without harm, but the bomb killed other people. Law enforcers would arrest him and charge him for murder. On the other hand, a law enforcer, carrying out his lawful duty, had to shoot a suicide bomber about to blow up an airport, which would cause the death of hundreds of individuals. Should the police officer be arrested for the murder of the terrorist, and face jail time too? Certainly not, that officer is a hero. Yet, he murdered someone. The officer knew what he was doing when he aimed his gun, just as how the suicide bomber knew what he was doing when he strapped himself with the explosive device.

Who would win this opposing argument? The individual who can provide substantial proof in quality or quantity of the facts.

The individual that would present the claim to support the person who stopped the bomber would win the debate; because the quantity and authenticity of evidence that is available. His swift actions saved hundreds of lives, prevent damage to properties that could surmount to millions of dollars, he saved businesses from losing valuable employees, he saved families from losing a loved one, and he also helped in preventing the disruption of visitors to his country that will have a positive impact on his country's economy.

A very common false equivalency is to assume that every time you see a male with a long beard and a head wrap, he is a Taliban.

Sometimes two actions might look identically without the facts and in such an instance; it can be easy for one to become a victim of false equivalency. However, if there is little or no evidence to support an argument false equivalency cannot exist. In order words, false equivalency, can only occur when there is a passing semblance in support; nevertheless, when detail scrutiny is conducted there is a vast difference between the quality, and or the quantity of evidence presented.

In a debate, you must present facts to support your claim. To garner facts, you must conduct detailed researches, and cross reference your findings to ensure that you will not fall prey to someone's false equivalency when being exhibited as fact.

Analyze the credibility of the source you are collecting data for your research from, and searching for at least three other reliable articles with the same information as the first source. By cross checking for other articles it can help you to ascertain if the information you are garnering for your research is accurate.

I know things are warming up now, but you are still doing great. So, continue reading. Remember, knowledge gives you power to excel in your craft.

CHAPTER 4

THE DIFFERENCE BETWEEN
FACT & OPINION

Congratulations! Thanks for making it to chapter four. You are such a great reader. I believe that you are tall, medium build, and you just winked one of your eyes. You are sitting having a snack and you are in sitting near a window while reading these words on your favorite electronic device. You purchased this book over the internet, because you want to learn how to debate or communicate more effectively. I think in the next five minutes a spider will crawl over your leg, while a fly will pitch on your window sill, a dog will bark at cat, and the cow will jump over the moon then land on its back.

Well, I do not know how much of what I have written above is factual; because I have absolutely no idea who you are, where you are from, how you ended up being able to read this book, and why you have chosen to read this book. I definitely know that the cow cannot jump over the moon. I am simply sharing my opinions with you.

An article written with some facts mixed with opinion is the most challenging. It will not always be as clear cut as what I have written above to distinguish between what is the fact and what is opinion.

When you find yourself at a cross roads trying to decide between fact and opinion then you must ask yourself some crucial questions such as: "Can this be proven?" "How many other individuals have proven this?" "Are the sources of information credible?" "How long ago was research conducted on this?" "Is the source experts in the field of study?"

Once something can be proven with no form of doubt perhaps it is a fact. Like England have a queen and a prime minister. The United States of America has a president. You have a surname. An ocean is a large body of water. All those statements are facts because they can be proven to be correct.

Some writers will let you know they are stating their opinion or thought on the particular topic by writing; "In my opinion..." "It is my belief..." "I hold the view..." "My perspective..." "Personally speaking or speaking personally..." "Based on my understanding..." "My subjective..."

Some statements that will let your opinion be conveyed in more convincing manner:

"Speaking, from personal experience that (state your claim to the motion) is of exceptional quality."

"Personally, I have discovered (state your perception) to be factual."

"I have had the opportunity to interact with a lot of people over the years, and never once have I ever heard anyone expressed that (state your opponent's claim) is the paramount format of ..."

In a debate the facts are a big deal. When you debate using facts from credible sources it shows you have thoroughly, prepared yourself for the debate. You are more capable of identifying false equivalency. You will know when your opponent is sharing an opinion. It will assist you to anticipate your competitor's argument and manipulate their arguments for your benefit. It will assist you to deliver your argument more accurately; because you are confident about the information you are presenting.

So, it is imperative you learn how to conduct detailed research to appropriately differentiate what articles are facts, from what articles are a journalist or writer's opinion. If you cannot find at least three or four articles, written by different individuals, who are expert researchers from credible institutions my advice to you is continue searching until you find facts.

Some statements that will convince others of the facts you are presenting:

"This is not a mere case of me uttering my opinion. I am stating this because it is a fact. (Then you share your claim of the motion)"

"The figures have certainly, conveyed the true story. (State your claim of the motion) is irrefutably the highest valued alternative obtainable."

(State the opposing team's claim) is impossible to achieve; because history has recorded its ineffectiveness (state the evidence of past attempts that failed regarding the opposing team's claim.)"

One last fact I will share with you, and that is, you have come to the end of this chapter.

CHAPTER 5

THE DIFFERENCE BETWEEN SUBJECTIVE & OBJECTIVE

Objective Information

Here is some food for thought - I left my home yesterday, no one was there, and one of my picture frames fell from the wall. Did it make a sound when it fell on the ground?

The fact that the picture frame fell from the wall, and made a sound is objective information. It can be proven that the picture fell from the wall, and the fact that it fell from the wall, it must have made a sound. Regardless that no one was there to hear or see what happen, it does not change the facts of what happened to the picture frame. It fell to the ground, and the impact of the frame hitting the floor must create a sound.

Objective information or data is facts. It is free from personal bias; because it is not powered by feelings or opinions. Objective information is measurable or observable. It is quantifiable.

If I wrote that one in every sixty-eight births, in the United States, has been recognized to have the autism spectrum and that three and half million individuals, living with the disorder of the autism spectrum. This is objective information; because it's proven to be authentic with facts, and statics. The evidence to prove this can be garnered from the government websites for disorders such as Center for Disease Control and Prevention (CDC). You can utilize information from other autism research official organizations websites as well.

Objective information can be sourced from news reporting writings or journals, textbooks, and encyclopedias.

Never forget when asked to provide objective information, you are to present facts. Facts which evidence can be provided through using quantitative reports, and other research mechanisms.

Subjective Information

Everyone in the world has a thirty-two-inch flat screen television, and everyone also enjoys watching the news.

Everyone in the world knows what an iPhone is, and can use the features of an iPhone.

The above statements are subjective information; because it contains personal feelings, and it cannot be proven to be factually true.

Subjective information is not absolute truth, and it cannot be mathematically defined, just as in the scenario created above. It is impossible to tell if everyone in the world has a thirty-two-inch flat screen television, who enjoy watching the news, and that everyone has an iPhone, and knows how to use the features.

Therefore, subjective information or perspective is based on emotions, feelings, personal interpretation and judgment. Subjective information is derived from one own understanding with an attempt to verify that interpretation by establishing a system of thought or feelings.

Take for instance the situation of the picture frame falling from the wall. If I had asked you; "What do you think happened to my picture frame?" I am introducing your feelings or opinion in the argument. You were not there when the picture frame got damaged; therefore, there is no way you can tell me for certain what happen to the picture frame.

I wanted you to think that flat screen television and iPhone is a common asset of everyone in the world. My statement evoked the thought in your mind if that could be true, but with no evidence to support my claim, it was very clear that I made a subjective view point. Subjective information might differ from individual to individual because it has to do with their emotions or inner thoughts.

Now that we have identified subjective information as a belief or an assumption, it is time to state where you usually find subjective information.

You can find subjective information on social media sites (comments), blogs, editorials, newspapers, and biographies.

Subjective information is not suitable to be used for reporting and making a concise decision.

We can comfortably state that objective and subjective are adjectives, which are channels to two ways of knowing.

Some objective information:

The moon is in the sky.

Anyone that is not blind can look at the moon in the sky.

Stars appear in the sky at night.

The Earth is a planet.

Oxygen is invisible, but without oxygen, we would suffocate and die.

A drink is a form of liquid.

Droplets of rain can be caught in a container.

Your body weight can be calculated in pounds or kilograms.

Some subjective information:

Ford Motor Company makes the best trucks.

The sun will fall from the sky one day.

One day humans will grow wings.

Kobe Bryant is the greatest basketball player ever.

I believe I could become a great doctor.

Can you tell which scenario below is objective and which is subjective?

Every woman knows how to cook and do house chores. The best meal to have on a Sunday is soup, and that is served in every household around the world. All men have a black tie, and all females own a pair of red shoes.

You have read an introduction and four chapters in *Debating To Win Arguments*. Debating To Win Arguments is a book written to help individuals become better debaters. There are over four chapters in the book.

Now if you had guessed that situation one is subjective, and scenario two is objective, then you were correct. And, I can proudly say I taught you the difference between subjective and objective information.

CHAPTER 6

HOW TO DISSECT OPPOSING VIEW

In a debate, there are two sides to the motion. Actually, none of the sides have more rights to the motion than the other initially; however, the arguments presented will give an edge to one team. The side that can put forth arguments with facts to support their interpretation of the motion, and to skillfully attack the opposing team's interpretation, to create doubt in the facts they had presented, is the team most likely declared the winner of the debate.

A debate team's pot of gold is to have an opposing team, with a quirky interpretation of the motion. Or for a more formal statement, if the opposing team only used subjective arguments in their interpretation, then, your team can easily use objective information to demonstrate falsehood in their interpretation. However, to accomplish that your team must have conducted detailed research, and armed with a wealth of in-depth information.

But there will be no silver lining if two debate teams have valid and viable interpretations of the motion. The presentation of many objective arguments, and presenting those arguments in a convincing manner, is exactly how your debate team might be declared the winner in such a case.

If a team has a rational interpretation of the motion, but present weak arguments to support their interpretation that team will lose points, due to low marks in the argument section, and might lose the debate.

Before you can learn how to dissect your opposing team views, you must master the preparation of your arguments.

Preparation of Your Argument

Let us examine how you should prepare your argument you can remember complicated information and how to structure your arguments.

The first step is that it is imperative you comprehend how to write clear and significant points. These points must be easy for you to understand. Therefore, you must take the time to summarize the points. Utilizing some visual illustrations and verbal illustrations can assist you to understand your complex information. They can also better connect with your audience;

because they too will understand the speech you are presenting.

It is crucial to understand that even though visual illustrations are props to help your arguments; you must take keen note that the visual illustrations are to *help* what other outstanding objective information you are presenting. If you have no good argument, then visual illustration can do little for you.

Verbal illustration can be used in four formats. Each format will assist you to present your arguments more effectively if used properly - especially complex argument.

The four different verbal illustrations are examples, metaphors, analogies, and anecdotes.

An *example* is one portion of an item or information, that is used to characterize a group as a whole. Examples are used to help others comprehend what they do not understand, or what they do not already know.

An a*nalogy* is making a contrast between two things typically to explain or to clarify a point. *Analogy* are of two formats namely, correspondence and inferences.

Correspondence refers to the similarity between two things that commonly would appear to be dissimilar. Like apples and oranges, which they often say you cannot compare, but both provide nutritional values. Both provide us with vitamins A, B1, and C. Both are citrus fruits. Some apples are round like the orange, and both are sometimes green. An apple can be made into a refreshing fruit juice, and an orange can also use to make a refreshing fruit juice. Apples can rot, and oranges can also rot. You must pick oranges from a tree, and you must pick apples from a tree. Apples have seeds, and oranges have seed.

Looking at an orange and an apple they are dissimilar; therefore, you would not think they could have so many things in common. However, through research and a lot of *correspondence* can be found between the two fruits. By stating their similarities, they do not appear that different to you now.

That is how you would use *correspondence* to explain your complex points to your audience. You find something which is easy to understand. Even though at a glance, it would seem different from whatever you must compare it with, but it has a lot of similarities with your complex arguments when you research them in detail. Use either the word *"like"* or *"as"* when describing the correspondence.

Deriving at a conclusion based on evidence and reasoning is defined as *interference*. The best way to explain *interference* is thinking about it as a ripple effect. An action in one area, can or will generation a reaction in another area. Consider if the cost of gasoline is increased the cost for your electricity bill would also increase. If the cost of gasoline is decreased the cost for your electricity bill would also decrease.

Use *interference* when you want to highlight the consequence(s) of an action. Whether it will generate a positive or negative reaction based on your claim of the motion.

When you want to peak your audience interest or inject them with humor, you use *anecdotes*. *Anecdotes* are interesting, brief summation, and or humorous occurrences of a situation.

Yes, you should not just bore your audience; let your speech come alive. Let them have to remember you after you speak. After all, debate is a friendly game.

The last analogy is *metaphors*. A *metaphor* is a figure of speech in, which a word or phrase is used in conjunction with an object or action, to which it is not literally applicable. Metaphors are like symbols or representation of something else.

An example of a *metaphor* in a phrase would say; "I raced with the hand of time." Another metaphor is "There is a fire in my soul." You cannot literally light a fire in your soul, and you cannot run with the hand of time. The metaphor adds more profound meaning to what you are trying to describe. The words also assisted in creating an image in your mind, and you can understand better what the person is trying to explain. The same manner in which the images are created in your mind, and you can understand more clearly what is being explained with metaphors; will cause the same reaction from your audience, when you incorporate metaphors in your explanations.

Since we have strained virtual illustration, and visual illustration, along with their usage, it is time to continue learning how to prepare your arguments.

When preparing for your debate you must keep storing materials that will be relevant in constructing your arguments. You can bookmark pages with information you plan to use or a page you want to review at a later time to see if that information will enhance your arguments. Another source of useful information is textbooks, so you would want to have them close by too. Sourcing information from newspapers and magazines can assist as well.

Conduct your form of analysis by speaking to other individuals expert in the field of your topic or who might have some experience. The information you garner from speaking to other persons ensure you find evidence to substantiate whatever information they will share with you.

Develop the healthy habit of notes taking, and recording ideas. It can prove beneficial to you, if you can also record your interviews with the individuals, you will speak to. It is actually very helpful to observe expert presenters and assess how they deliver their arguments. Take keen note of their tone, when they change the volume, and pitch of their voices. How they gesticulate, and how they keep engaging their audience through eye contact.

Create a folder with the information you have compiled to write your speech. Ensure you have the four types of analogy in your file to create balance and the production of an effect speech. Evaluating your material is a must. This is how you will separate what is relevant from what is irrelevant. Arrange your points from the least important to the most important for last. People often remember what is said last; therefore, you want them to remember your crucial points. A part of the evaluation is recording yourself, and then playing back the recording to discover areas you need to improve on in your delivery tactics.

Another helpful tool when constructing your speech is a dictionary to improve your vocabulary. It is not about being ostentatious, but sometimes things sound better using a synonym of a word. For example, instead of saying; "It is not about you being a show-off." Stating "It is not about being ostentatious," sounds better and less colloquial. Being too colloquial can damage your argument in a debate. Effective formal communication is often free of colloquial expressions, or they are not used frequently.

Using cue cards to record your notes in big writing and numbering each card is the best option for you when presenting your speech. Numbering the cards is a useful reminder of which points to be argued, and if for some unfortunate reason, your cue cards should fall to the ground, and scatter on the day of your presentation; they can easily and quickly, be replaced in their correct order. When you are very skilled, you can have the cue cards in the palm one of your hands, and you occasionally glimpse at the cards switch a card to the back of the pile when finished with it.

Honestly, I would only suggest that you use the method of placing the cue cards in the palm of your hands if there is no podium for you to stand behind when presenting. Once there is a podium, place your pile of cue cards on it. Take an occasionally peek at the one at the top, and while you are speaking on the last point on the card at the top, you use one hand to remove it, to place it face down on the pile you will create for cue cards, which you have used already. Removing the cue card from one pile to another takes a few seconds allowing you to keep eye contact with your audience, and continue speaking as you are doing so.

A second reason for placing the cue cards on the podium is that your hands will be free to gesticulate and use your props you would have taken to help heighten your delivery.

The third reason for the cue cards on the podium, and using the cards demonstrate that you know what you are delivering, and it forces you to know your material too. To deliver a convincing speech you must know your material thoroughly.

It is imperative to note that even though I had said that you should commence with your least important point, your first point must also be an attention grabber. Meaning, when you speak, if a member of the audience or the judge had his or her head down, making jottings of notes, they must stop, and look at you after hearing what you must say. So, you must start with a statement that is a bang. Similarly, to what newspapers do with the headlines they create for stories. These headlines are geared at getting readers attention so they have to purchase the paper to read the story in its entirety. Then you guarantee your audience remembers you by ending on a convincing, and note even stronger than what you had started with.

Everything about the delivery of your speech must be structured to the key, including your voice. You cannot speak too softly, and not too quickly either. You must create a balance. This balance only comes after you have recorded and timed yourself speaking, and finding expert speakers with a similar sounding voice like you, then observe how they use their voice will assist you to accomplish this feat.

If you are wondering when will you learn how to dissect opposing view, well everything I have been telling is in preparation and anticipation of your opponent's views. You cannot dissect what you do not know. Even if you hear your opponent make an argument you think you should or can dissect; you cannot do so with false equivalency, subjective view, or opinion, these will make your argument weak and not credible.

Arguing your side effectively means that you understand the view point of the opposing team, and that is how you can dissect their arguments. Therefore, when conducting your research, you must gather information to support your views, and information to support the opposing side view. By looking at things from both sides of the coin, you are in a better positon to construct your arguments, and dissecting rebuttals of the opposing team from the get-go. The probe in the depths of your knowledge will be demonstrated successfully; when you can weaken your opposing team arguments before they even present them.

I do not know if you are like me, but I like to ask a lot of questions. I have a curious mind. Some individuals would want you to perceive that having a curious mind means that you are inquisitive, and just want to pry into other peoples' personal affairs. Well, I am not going to totally dismiss that what they claim is not factual; sometimes I ask a question to pry. Have we not all done so at some point in our life?

But honestly, usually I just cannot resist the urge to learn more. Looking at things from the other person's perspective allow me to understand that person's beliefs better. Seeking answers to my questions will provide me with more information, about the situation at hand.

Great debaters have curious minds, or lacking a formal term, they are critical thinkers. Critical thinking is defined as; *"Intellectually disciplined process of actively and skillfully conceptualizing, applying, analyzing, synthesizing, or evaluating information gathered from, or generated by, observation, experience, reflection, reasoning, or communication as a guide to belief and action."* according to the *"U.S. National Council for Excellence in Critical Thinking."*

Now based on that long definition, you know without a doubt that critical thinkers ask a lot of questions. Critical thinkers look at things from all conceivable angles. A critical thinker will even create a third and fourth side to ensure they are covering all probable angles. There is absolutely no way you can profess to know a topic when you cannot speak about it from the supporting side and the opposing side.

To be certain that you can dissect any opposing argument, you must conduct detailed research. Search for information to support the topic, and to oppose the topic. This means you must dig deep and wide to saturate your mind with all the information you can find on the topic.

Having in-depth knowledge on a topic is your greatest secret weapon of winning a debate. With knowledge comes confidence and comfort to speak.

Have you ever met a sales representative of a particular product, and after listening to their sale pitch, you end up purchasing a product you had no intention of purchasing, and probably do not even need?

Then you are left asking yourself; "How did I get tricked into purchasing something I do not need?"

If you have never figured out the answer to that question, I will assist you now in finding a response to your question. You purchased the item from the sales representative because of the skillful art of persuasion. That sales representative was ready to dissect your "No", and he or she armed themselves with information about all the possible reasons you might say "No" to him or her.

Persuasion and information made it possible to achieve the sale. If you tell a sales representative you cannot afford a product; that representative will let you know that his or her company understands the financial constraints that individuals are experiencing, and that is why they have come up with a limited time offer. He or she further explains how the product can alleviate special needs to save you time and money. Their description of the product will be so convincing that you will think they know you personally to be suggesting ways the product could be used in your daily life. After purchasing the product, you might or might never use the product, but because you had purchased it willingly, you do not want to return it. So, you decide to just keep the product.

Debating works in a similar format. Think of yourself as the sales representative. The judges or audience, is the person you will be selling your product to. However, the opposing team is a competitor in your market trying to snatch your prospective customer by finding faults with the product you are offering. So, you study your competitor's product to discover fallacy with their product and the benefits of their product to your prospective customers. You already know what your competitor will use as their sales pitch to discredit your product, and since it is your product, you already know everything about it. So you dissect their arguments using all the information you have, and with persuasion, you can convincingly sell your product by creating the belief that your product is the most superior merchandise.

You will not be nervous if you are knowledgeable about your topic, and you will persuasively present your speech.

A persuasive phrase or a phrase to dissect your opponent's view is a simple indirect method, which you can use to highlight the opposing team's arguments as inferior to your arguments.

Here are some ways you can begin your argument to dissect your opponent's views:

"(State the opposing team's claim to the motion here) will lead to detrimental consequences for all stakeholders. We can certainly, resolve this by simply going with (state your claim here) in the first place."

"My opponent might have had constructed more (state the competitor's argument here), but that is because (stat will use opponent's product here) did not do their research..."

"We definitely do not need (state opposing team idea); because (state your claim) already addresses that..."

"You might believe what you want, but (state your claim to the motion) is the best option."

"(State the opposing team claim) certainly appears to be a good concept when taken at face value, but our (state your argument) provides more versatility and is more cost effective."

"I'm sure the opposition has convinced some of you that their argument is best, but they have not been candid with you."

You also must use persuasive words to address your audience or the judges.

Here are some persuasive words you might use to address your audience or the judges:

These words will express confidence and positivity in your speech.

Precise, precisely, accurate, accurately, assertively, emphatically, unequivocally, undeniably, categorically, definite, definitely, absolutely, one-hundred percent, affirmatively, yes, clearly, central, and strongly

You the words below when you are ready to put the nail in your opponent's arguments:

Vicious, atrocity, atrocious, appalling, dreadful, befuddling, confusing, cruel, detrimental, harmful, inferior, despicable, contemptible, outrageous, astonishing, astounding, shocking, reprehensible, shameful, belligerent, pugnacious, offensive, obnoxious, detestable, abhorrent, repugnant, repulsive, hideous, horrible, unstable, austere, ascetic, severe, no

Finally, there are three different speakers. The emotional speaker is guided by feelings and speaks from the heart. Most of the great raconteurs are emotional speakers. There is the speaker who speaks from the mouth, and never carefully, thinks about what he or she will utter; this person only likes the sound of his or her voice. Then, you have the speaker who speaks from the head, but even though they have a lot of facts to share, they tend to very monotonous.

What kind of speaker should you become out of the three types?

Truthfully, you should not try to be just one type. You must create a balance between all three. You can like the sound of your voice when you have worked on your pitch and volume. However, you must speak from your head and not just babble your mouth away. You do not want to be boring, so even though you are speaking from your head, you must put your heart into it. Whatever is done from the heart will touch the soul of other people's heart too.

Persuasion is useful not only during a debate but can always be utilized in other aspect of our lives. It can be used when you want to enter a business transaction. When being interviewed for a job, and when being interviewed to gain entry into an academic institution. It can even be used when trying to win someone's heart. An articulate and persuasive speaker will always incite the undivided attention of his or her audience.

CHAPTER 7

STATISTIC & HOW THEY CAN BE MANIPULATED

S tatistics have been manipulated by almost everyone. Even in our conversation with close friends, we refer to statistics, though more in an informal manner. Take, for example, you are talking to a friend, and the friend said to you; "I did not know you like chocolate cake?" Then, you respond by saying; "All females love chocolate cake."

Really, all females love chocolate cake? Because you certainly do not know every female on this planet. So, how does every female love chocolate? How can you prove it?

People often manipulate statistics to make their arguments more convincing to others. How often have you heard someone say; "I had a million reasons..." "I had a million opportunities..." "I had like, a million friends..." And the list can be continued of how often people have used figures in their attempt to convince others of their point.

However, I do not believe that any one can surpass politicians in the manipulation of statistics. Politicians, more than anyone else, have manipulated statistics in their bid to sell us that they are the best candidate to improve the economy, and help us have a better life.

We have all been tricked by the politician's manipulation of statistics to gain our trust and support. Even if we do not literal go to the polls to vote for them, we engage in debates about them, and state our opinion why he or she is a better candidate; based on the manipulated statistics plans they shared.

If a lie is repeated long enough, it will become the belief to some people. Technology has aided many in spreading their manipulated statistics. Using the right headlines and inserting a few graphs stating that based on a study, which was conducted recently, in a university in the state of... or in the city of... it has been revealed that....

Just like wild fire, the data will be all over different social media websites. Some individuals might take the time to research if there is any merit to the claim put forth; but sadly, the *majority* will not do so.

But what exactly is statistic?

According to Dictioinary.com, *Statistics* is the branch of mathematics dealing with numerical data – mode, mean, median, normal distribution curve, sample, standard deviation, and statistical significance. The estimation of exact values of parameters from a sample of data is a specific function of statistics.

Therefore, statistics involves three main steps. The first step is the collection of the numerical data. Second, the analyzing of the information collected. Third, is interpreting the information. The information collected is known as the sample, and the sample is collected from a population. The word population, when used in statistics, is not necessarily referring to people. For example, if a research was being conducted in the area with the most alligators in Florida. Then Florida would be the population. The alligators being research would be the sample.

We have been fed a lie for many years, and that fib is that the numbers cannot lie. The numbers do lie; because humans can manipulate them to sway an argument in their favor.

How Are The Numbers Manipulated?

Inadequate Statistics Information

Frequently, we will hear someone quoting percentage of a study, but seldom do we hear the total population studied. To validate a relative claim, statistics is often used to do so; for example, 90% prefer cookies and cream ice cream. However, the statistics had not mentioned the sample size. I wonder why? Let us now examine why sample size was not mentioned.

If you place two socks in a box, one pair is red, and the other pair is blue you would have a 50% chance of selecting either a blue or red socks from the box. If you repeat the exercise six times out of those six attempts, you picked the red socks five times, and the blue socks once. You would be accurate in stating that 16% of the time you selected the red socks. Now, you were contracted by Company A to conduct the research to discover how many individuals would prefer a red over blue socks. By reporting that 16% prefer the blue socks over the red socks, and not stating the sample size you had used; you are manipulating the statics. The fact, that you did not conduct the research, with a large enough sample size, and stated that to Company A, means you manipulated the statistics.

The Rule of Averages

From an early age, we learn about rounding off numbers and finding averages. Statistics can be calculated for almost everything; for the places people visit the most, the cost to visit those places, or the average sale of a particular item. Some averages you would read about in statistics are for examples, they could state average amount spent by individuals to visit Paris is $10,000, or the average beds sold in January is 1025. But, even averages can be manipulated to for the benefit of those presenting the information. Take for example the organization you are working sent a report stating that their salary is very competitive when compared to the salary of other businesses in the same industry. In the report, it stated that the average salary of the manager and the supervisors amounted to $200,000, but a detailed examination of all the salaries would reveal that manager of the company was paid $250,000,000 for the year, while the supervisors were paid only $50,000 or less sometimes for the year. In such a case your organization would have manipulated the statistics to allow employees to think that they are in a better position than employees of the competitor's company. To refute such a case, you must find the median or the middle value, which would more accurately state the true amount being paid as salary.

Graphs Used To Display A Picture of Accuracy

So, you have seen a lot of graphs, displaying statistical information, and you think that in no way these can be manipulated; because you have a literal view of the numbers. Well, I am about to burst your bubble; because graphs can be manipulated too.

So, you are given a graph and you are looking at all the variables, which are very impressive, based on the statistics report conducted. But, what you are not aware of, is that statistic report is manipulated to reveal something far more favorable than what the figures are in reality. You must analyze the scale used in the data. The scale is often time altered to achieve impressive results for statistic reports, which are submitted in a graph format.

Watch out for Percentages and Percentage Points

There is an actual difference between *percentages* and *percentage points*. Those presenting statistics reports in percent value capitalize on the fact that most people will not take the time to examine if it is a percentage or percentage point being used in the report.

A percentage is calculated from the whole of the item. This whole does not necessarily have to be 100, where as a percentage point is a unit of measurement calculated from a portion of one hundred (100).

Let me put an example in for you to grasp the difference between percentage point (percent point), and percentage. You read a company that produces toaster ovens statistic report on faulty equipment. In February, the company sold seventy-five toaster ovens. But, unfortunately, forty or 53% of the fifty-two toasters ovens, which were sold in February, were returned by customers; because they were faulty. In the industry – those that produce toaster ovens – the average for faulty toasters is 45%; therefore, that business presents a statistic report stating that their faulty toasters were only 8% higher than the industry average for faulty toasters.

Truthfully, they know that it was 8 percentage points higher, but 17.8% higher than the industry average.

Let me break it down further for you. Remember that percentage points are not calculated based on the whole (100), but only calculated from a portion of the whole. However, the 8-percentage points higher is due to calculating using the based figure 45. Therefore, to calculate the percentage difference, you must divide 8 by 45, then, multiply that answer by 100. Your final answer would reveal that they had 17.8% higher faulty toaster ovens than the industry's average for faulty toaster ovens.

So, a percentage point or percent point is the difference between two percentages, or the arithmetic difference in units of two percentages. For example, if something moves from

21% to 22% it has a rise of 1 percentage point. You must only minus the percentage of what the item was at first, to what percentage it moved up to, in order to find the percentage point.

Manipulation Of The Sampling

Statistic reports can be manipulated long before the information is presented. The report can be manipulated from the sampling stage to ensure that a certain result is recorded. This manipulation of the sample is *sample bias*. The sample can be biased by selection of a particular area, self-selection, leading question bias, and social desirability bias.

Let us now examine sampling bias more closely:

Area Bias

A statistic report which stated that quails, one bird hunted mostly, is now becoming extinct and should be listed as an endangered species. That was not stated in the statistic report in the area the study was conducted. This study was not conducted in all areas that quails could be found, but only in two areas that quails are used in hunting games a lot. If the area of study was expanded, the study would have revealed that internationally, the birds are not in extinction.

It might have been that the person who conducted the research felt that bird hunting is wrong, or it might have been that they just simply did not take the time to conduct detailed research. But that individual had committed area bias, and the statistic report was manipulated.

The area of sample must be an adequate representation of the population to be analyzed.

Self-selection Bias

The individuals selected to participate in the study possess certain traits that correlate with the study, and therefore, that participant or sample is a non-representative sample.

Take, for example, you selected a focus group to garner their feedback about the latest footwear of a Company VVB, which is a sandal. The individuals you selected for the focus group are people who do not like sandals. They only wear shoes with heels. By selecting only individuals that wear shoes with heels, they could not give the feedback someone that only wore sandals could provide. Adversely, if you only selected people who wore sandals you still would have engaged in self-selection bias. The sample must be free from bias and should be conducted among various individuals.

Leading Question Bias

Just as the statement suggests, that is what occurs. The researchers ask participants a question that will solicit a particular answer from the individuals.

The researcher will structure the interview question with certain words such as; "Don't you think that pencils must be purchased with a sharpener?" By structuring the question in this manner, the tone of the researcher's question is suggesting what he or she believes the answer should be.

A more appropriate structure to the researcher's question that would not result in a leading question would be to ask the participant; "Pencils and sharpeners, can they be purchased together?" or "Do you think that pencils and sharpeners should be purchased together?" These questions are more open, and give room for the participant to answer the question asked of them. In this case, it would be what that participant believes, and not what the researcher wants him or her to say.

Social Desirability Bias

When a researcher knows that if he or she asks certain questions of a participant, he or she will not answer truthfully. If the participant answers truthfully, it would be a socially unacceptable behavior.

If you are conducting a survey in which you ask participants; "Have you ever eaten food after you had used the toilet, but you did not wash your hands before you eat?" or "Have you ever left your house, and did not brush your teeth?" Also, asking "Have you ever worn dirty clothes to work?" These are all examples of Social Desirability Bias.

I mean, come on, be realistic, who wants to air their dirty laundry in public, no matter how undesirable that participant's behavior is, that person will not want to admit those things to someone they do not know personally. There are times people attempt to hide their social undesirable behavior patterns from friends, and family, much less a complete stranger.

Therefore, it can be concluded that one tool to assist in manipulation of statistics reports is by creating bias in the sampling procedure.

Can the data analysis be manipulated too?

The answer to that question is a definite yes.

Data analysis is also called *data analytics*. This involves the scrutinizing, separation, converting, and the modeling of the data to highlight useful information, suggestions, conclusions and finding information that will support decision-making.

Here is how data analysis might be manipulated. A study was conducted about the sale of ice cream on a Sunday to discover what type is sold the most. The grid used is a bar chart with on its horizontal axis, is the different the ice cream, and on its vertical axis, the amount sold on Sundays.

Four different types were researched. The four types were bars, cones, popsicles, and tub ice creams.

The statics report presented to the board of directors showed that more individuals purchased popsicles on a Sunday. However, the data analysis revealed this information: 10 individuals purchased ice cream bars. 30 persons purchased cone ice creams. 15 people bought tub ice creams and 1 individual purchased 40 popsicles. The individual that purchased the popsicles ate them all by himself; he just loved popsicles.

Yes, more popsicles were sold on Sundays, but it was just one person making the purchase. What if something happened to that person, and he cannot eat popsicles anymore. Then, there would be no sale made for popsicles on a Sunday. By excluding from the statistic report it was just one gentleman purchasing the popsicles on a Sunday, the statistic report was manipulated. An accurate statistic report would display that cone ice creams are sold the most out of the four types on a Sunday, and that even though there is a record of 40 popsicles, it was purchased by just one person.

How To Identify Graphical Information That Has Not Been Manipulated

According to *Edward Tufte*, from the *"Visual Display of Quantitative Information, (Graphics Press 2001)"* **Graphical Excellence** is that which gives to the viewer the greatest number of ideas in the shortest time with the least ink in the smallest space.

Therefore, presentations must be well-made, comprising of data of substance, statistics, and design. The composite ideas should be communicated with lucidity, meticulousness, and efficiency. Good graphs done in a proper format using the right scale tells a story about the data.

When Validating Graphical Information:

You must try to discover the ulterior motive behind the statistic report. You cannot hold everything as fact just because it has the label of *Science and Data*.

The sources are very important when validating graphical information. So, look at the sources. If no sources were listed, **do not** trust the report.

Carefully, inspect if there is any possible source of bias in the data presented. Scrutinize how the data was collected, who collected the data, and where it was collected from.

Examine closely, the data legend of an axis and the data axis. Try to perceive if the data is representing percentages or percentage points.

What does all this information on manipulation of statics report have to do with debating?

Basically, everything when you think about it. Debate is mainly won on the convincing delivery of the facts or objective information. You garner facts and objective information from researches. Researches often contain statistical information.

When collecting information to structure your arguments, ensure that whatever information you will use to substantiate your claim has not been manipulated; because your opponent will be researching your claim of the motion too. The opponent plans on doing the same thing you are planning on doing to their argument. That is to identify subjective arguments, opinions, false equivalency, and manipulated statics reports.

Rebuttals will carry significant value when they can quickly, and clearly, identify fallacy in statistic reports. Also, your arguments will be substantiated more, when; you can dissect and use the manipulated static reports to refute the opposing team's arguments. As a skillful and well-learned debater, you can use the opposing team's logic against them, to further authenticate your claim of the motion.

CHAPTER 8

HOW TO USE OPPOSING ARGUMENT LOGIC AGAINST THEM

You have done your research. Your compiled your information. Your arguments are constructed, and you have your cue cards ready. With no further ado, it is the day of reckoning. The question waiting to be answered by all who are present is: "Who will deliver the facts, with consistency, in a convincing manner?"

We have heard that knowledge is power, and in the right hand can be a powerful tool. Let your hand hold the tool of knowledge, and control its power through the presentation of your speech.

In life, every positive has its negative; therefore, if having knowledge is power, the lack of it means you will be weak. If you understand your opponent and have the tool of knowledge, you can always weaken your opponent's arguments and even use their own logic against them.

Understanding how your opponent normally presents his or her argument can also assist you in your task to use their logic against them. Most debaters have a unique style of delivering. Know your opponent's unique style of presenting.

By researching your opposing team, you can better organize the members of your team, to decide who will counteract the different members of the opposition. And it will help your team to structure your speeches, as well to match, or supersede the presentation style of your competitor.

Consider the opposing team's logic as a dart. Their aim is to throw the dart of negative logic to damage the eye of your argument. But, you are going to skillfully catch that dart, and throw it right back at your opponent, to create the same damage in their claims, which they wanted to cause in your argument by throwing the dart at you.

Look at how to use the logic of your opposing team against them.

Your opponent is arguing the claim that animals should not be sacrificed for scientific experiments. They present their argument that the animals must endure undue duress, and sometimes even the loss of life in the bid of scientific experiments. They might even put forth the points that animals are subject to feeling pain just like humans; because they have brain cells and a nervous system.

You would reply with: "The claim my opponent has made is that animals can experience pain as humans. But, are my opponents suggesting that we resort to the inhumane action of injecting our fellow humans with chemicals to discover if the scientific research will succeed? Might, I further add that it is because of these very experiments that humans are still alive, a lot of medicines were discovered only after numerous tests in laboratories were conducted, with animals, used as the sample. Medicines, which my very opponents have benefited from using; I hope , my opponents, will be using no form of medicine that was discovered through scientific testing; because animals were samples. Could it also be that my opponents are proposing that we do nothing to save the lives of our brothers and sisters, who are suffering, having to endure undue duress from illnesses; an illness that some caught from carrying out the diligent care of an animal? I should hope not."

You must try to resolve any issues that the opposing team has raised before moving on. So, when an opponent presenting uses negative logic in their speech, at the beginning of his or her speech, opposing debater must address and try to dispel whatever issue the opponent had raised in their argument.

If you are debating as part of team ensure that your arguments flow. Though each member of the team will debate on a different strength of your claim to the motion, it must have correlation to the other teammates. After the debate, it must seem that you all tied your arguments together, which strengthen the points you have all presented on. Judging is conducted on the team and judges also look on individual speaker's performance. You must be able to connect your speeches to each other as an individual and help your team also to refute any logic that the opposing team has presented.

It is all about using the lemons thrown at you to make lemonade, but you cannot make the lemonade if you do not know, or you do not have the correct ingredients. It cannot be recommended or stressed enough that you must conduct detailed researches, and look at the motion from both sides of the coin or from all prospectives.

CONCLUSION

There are four "D's" that you must learn about when it comes on to debating.

First D – you must *defend* your claim to the motion.

Second D – you must aim to *dulcify* your opponent's negative arguments against your claim. This can be done through the combination of their negative logic, with some strong positive logic, and soothe away the damage they had intended to cause your claims to the motion.

Third D – you must *discredit* your opposing team's arguments by highlighting their false equivalency, manipulated data, and subjective arguments.

Fourth D – you must aim to *destroy* your competitor's arguments using facts and ethical logic.

In conclusion, research, research, research. It is important when you want to become a debater. Improve your vocabulary by keeping a dictionary or by developing the habit of learning at least two new words each day. Make sure you are informed of the latest news in the media, having a folder with newspaper reports can be very useful.

Study expert debaters to see what principles you might adopt from them. Always improve your communicating skills. Observe your own body language keenly when speaking to ensure that your body language is not conveying a negative message to your audience.

Practice the art of note taking concise notes; because you must make notes when conducting your research, and you must take notes when your opponents are speaking to know which points you must refute.

Create a balance in everything you too. Do not be too zealous or too over confident.

Be humble and willing to face any possible outcome of the game of debating. You can present your arguments in the best possible way, and still the judge might give the winning point to the other team. Do not get upset accept your lost and move on. The knowledge you will gain from entering debating competitions is a lifelong treasure. No one can take that knowledge from you. So, if you look at it from the perspective that you will be gaining knowledge, there are no losers in the game of debating. Everyone wins knowledge and experience.

By becoming a debater, you are equipping yourself with two very powerful tools that can be used in all aspect of your life. These two tools are articulate communicating skills, and the art of persuasion.

I rest my case my stating I hope you had enjoyed reading *Debating To Win Arguments* as much as I enjoyed sharing the information with you.

Thank you for taking the time to read and purchase my book.

SPECIAL REQUEST FROM THE AUTHOR

Enjoy This Book? You Can Make a Difference! Reviews are the most influential tool for getting attention for my books. Much as I would love to, I do not have the financial footing of a great publisher and I cannot take out full page ads in the newspaper. But with your help I can make my dream become a reality when you become a committed and loyal reader and encourage others to support my work.

Honest reviews of my books help bring them to the attention of other readers. If you have enjoyed this book I would be very grateful if you could spend just a minute or two leaving a review (it can be as short as you like) on the book's page.

Thank You so much.

~ The End~

47148073R00043

Printed in Poland
by Amazon Fulfillment
Poland Sp. z o.o., Wrocław